T0368631

Exalt

A book of Christian Poems

Brad McElroy

WestBow Press books may be ordered through booksellers or by contacting:

WestBow Press
A Division of Thomas Nelson & Zondervan
1663 Liberty Drive
Bloomington, IN 47403
www.westbowpress.com
844-714-3454

ISBN: 979-8-3850-3814-5 (sc)
ISBN: 979-8-3850-3813-8 (e)

Print information available on the last page.

WestBow Press rev. date: 11/26/2024

WESTBOW
PRESS®
A DIVISION OF THOMAS NELSON
& ZONDERVAN

Contents

Many thanks to my cousin Father David McElroy for inspiring and renewing my faith. This book is dedicated to him faithfully.

Other books written by the author

Emergence
Entangled
Embedded
Envelop
Eventual

Mercy

A blessing undeserved
For actions unbecoming
And thoughts reviled
To heal sins transgressing

Preserving holiness
From a fallen state
It restores body and soul
To a godly grace

Combining forgiveness,
Love, charity and hope
Parts unretractable blame
Into dissolving fears to cope

Unpredictable to men
Never the less to God
Mercy is eternally present
Given freely to all

Without it there is death
With it there is life
It is ours to ask
To end painful strife

Forgiveness

Fire in thoughts
Bitterness in heart
Harsh words heard
Peace torn apart

Instinct to fight
Mood to retaliate
Pride cut down
Emotion obliterated

Difficult to ignore
But take the higher road
Find a way and means
To make peace abode

Forgiveness isn't easy
But worth it in the end
To love neighbor as self
And compromise to bend

Praise

How do I praise you
God the Almighty
Who needs nothing at all
Humbly I proceed lightly

Protection that was given
Through many tough trials
Always guiding me safely
Thru the lows and the highs

I am at your debt
Never able to repay
For the love and mercy shown
On each and every day

What can I do
To show gratitude
To my Father
With his divine attitude

Only with my heart
To love him most dear
And submit to his will
Even when it's unclear

God

The mysterious Trinity
Forever in eternity
Three essences in one
To save with certainty
Bring grace upon us
Fire souls with passion
Correct disobedience
And grant mercy to creation
We submit to you freely
To receive the blessing
Of everlasting life
Your word being promising
That sin will be forgiven
Hearts renewed
Souls purified
As eternity ensues
We adore your glory
We praise your name
You are our savior
With hope you came
Let all be influenced
To fulfill your plan
And love one another
While being servants to man

Communion

Communion is a union
Between God and man
Entwining finite to eternity
Across all of Earth's lands
Body and blood
In the ultimate sacrifice
For our salvation
To cleanse sin's vice
Sacred is the bread
Revered is the wine
Both from Jesus
For all of time
Remember his sacrifice
On Calgary Hill
Where he gave up his life
So we could live still
Take it to honor him
His gift of love
For filial children
To ascend as doves
It is meant for all
The strong and meek
The rich and poor
All who heavenly seek

The Fall

Eat from the tree Eve
You surely won't die
You will be like God
Knowing all in the sky
As you say, I will do
It is a beautiful fruit
So delicious to bite
To the tongue it suits
Adam, share in my delight
Taste before the night
We will have knowledge of all
And retain such might
What have you done Eve
Death surely will come upon you
But I will stay by your side
And I begin to chew
Where are you my children
Why do you hide
And why cover your loins
My command you did not abide
You two will be cursed
And sent into exile
To sweat and toil on earth
With your life ending in a long last sigh

Guilt

Gut wrenching
Body aching
Thoughts troubling
Heart breaking

Knowing right from wrong
And making the choice
To decide on the latter
Regret will be hoist

No turning back
Beating the chest
Slapping the face
Living not with the best

Memory sears
Every detail remembered
How could it of happened
Guilt is delivered

Only one solution
Confess and forgive
Time will heal all
Never do it again

Pride

The most demonic sin
And the first sin ever
Making Satan fall from grace
To be permanently severed

Narcissism is its core
Ones ego inflated
To exalt and boast
About oneself highly created

Opposite of humility
It separates one another
Until the flock is apart
And unity has no brothers

Pride is vulgarly vain
With little justification
Individuals flaunt
Lacking spiritualization

Be always on guard
With yourself and others
To avoid this attitude
And pick wisely another

Lust

A consuming desire
Of sexual nature
Burns the flesh
And makes one a slave later

Always thirsting
For orgasmic pleasure
Fornicating constantly
To treat flesh as treasure

An unforgiven drive
For genital satisfaction
Can cause destruction
Of holy reactions

Chasing sex constantly
With a nature of lust
Contributes to sin
And makes love unjust

Gluttony

Eating is a must
To keep the body strong
For vitality and health
It is a conditioned longed

But too much is bad
Overindulging hurts
With overconsuming food
Diseases can lurk

Not to mention the waste
From eating more and not less
That could have been given to the poor
But not because some eat best

Without spirituality
Eating can be ravenous
Missing the higher call
Gorging will sadden us

Feast conservatively
And protect from excess
Life will be long and well
Doctors all profess

Greed

Nothing ever enough
Desiring more and more
Constantly consuming
Creates material scores

Striving for excess
Coveting all in sight
Wishing for this and that
Never satisfied by night

Stuck in this mire
Goods become God
Earthly idols are worshipped
But they are all frauds

If one is very selfish
If one denies charity
Then lose your greed
And see with better clarity

Sloth

Overindulgence in apathy
And an idleness of time
No inclination to work
Obligations become a crime

Nowhere finding ambition
Lost is motivation
Laziness is in exclamation
Lethargy finding satisfaction

Progress slows to a halt
Care for others illusive
Sloth makes one dull
And toward the will abusive

Muster up the energy
To engage in fruitfulness
Stay out of stagnation
And rather head toward usefulness

Envy

Ignoring accomplishments
Jealous of others success
Failing to realize
What could be the best

Missing all gratitude
Without a compliment
Shaming praise deserved
Dishonors a supplement

It is a soar and prideful vice
Which focuses on spite
One needs true reflection
In order to make it right

What others do for fame
Is not to be blamed
But instead it's a blessing
Sometimes honoring God's name

Wrath

Anger fully unbridled
Seeking hateful vengeance
Drains the heart of love
Prosecuting a sentence

Wishing others to suffer
Emotions of strong wrath
Desires all misfortune
In a negative hurtful class

A sense of justification
For a wrong endured
Can cause evil thoughts
Of harm or death to incur

It is extremely antisocial
Considered very grave
Escaped from all holy mercy
Making the mood a dark day

Do Unto Others

It is better to give
Than it is to receive
A lasting moral principle
That should be believed

Denying oneself some
For the benefit of others
Brings charity to life
And the singular to multiple color

Treat people fairly
And forgive them their sins
As God has forgiven yours
As said in prayer of long been

Conflict can be resolved
By understanding another's position
Peace can come about
And be brought to fruition

Love also can be shown
Abundantly given
When caring for others
Is unselfishly not hidden

Hope

Hope is priceless
Essential to have
It carries us thru trials
Consoling on our behalf
Without it there's despair
And troubles are grave
No future looks bright
Pessimistic natures behave
With it one can cope
In days to years
Coming tribulations
Are soothed from doubts and fears
An outlook of assurance
Tilting the mind to trust
And knowing a reprieve
Can turn bad into just
Diligently exercised
Grace will abound in thought
Troubles will be temporary
And bright futures will be sought

Peace

A gentle soft overflow
Of true lasting comfort
Bears real tranquility
Making stillness convert

To a sense of steady calm
Steering the mind benign
Whispering like a breeze
Over a running stream's shine

Convincing true sedation
That forbears a repose
Brings an ease to mind
Of all that is proposed

Good for restful outlooks
A state of lasting peace
Envelopes the heart's soul
And heals with total ease

Faith

Something not seen
Or proven with facts
But believed as truth
Confidence never lacks

Influenced by the eternal
With promises to bear
A blessing for mankind
That more is truly there

Letting go of skepticism
Letting go of doubt
Models heavenly belief
Of a future place to scout

To heaven high above
Waiting for our souls
In trust they are accepted
Converted to holy molds

To some with disbelief
It's considered folly
But for those truly convicted
It's a powerful accurate volley

Nativity

As Gabriel told Mary
She would conceive a son
By mystery of the Holy Spirit
To unite the world in one

In the town of Bethlehem
On a star lit night
Jesus was born
In a manger with dim light

A baby so delicate
And so vulnerable
All human in appearance
With the divine later discoverable

An infant for now
To become savior of the world
Ready to fulfill prophesy
And resist temptations hurled

Celebrate and remember
His birth on this day
And give Holy thanks
For his preaching that swayed

Resurrection

Sentenced to die
Nailed to a cross
For mankind's sins
That made them lost

On that Friday day
He gave up his life
Prosecuted unjustly
With the ruled rife

He fulfilled all signs
Of being Israel's savior
Proving to be God's son
And starting new behaviors

He rose Sunday morning
After the break of dawn
To a new and glorious body
With death being forever gone

To all who believe
And follow Jesus's way
Life will be eternal
In all of Heaven's days

Printed in the United States
by Baker & Taylor Publisher Services